BODY LANGUAGE

THE SECRET FOR PERSUASION ALL PEOPLE

Joe Cooper

On September 27, I managed to reach a total of 1700 people who started following my education.

Marco and I want to thank you for becoming one of us, and we have a surprise for you.

I'm writing to you to let you know that if you buy the paper version, you will have the free kindle version of this book for you and for anyone you want.

I am doing it because I want as many people as possible to approach these concepts to understand how manipulation and body language work.

So, if you know people who would be interested in the subject who are curious and eager to learn new things, don't wait to give them this book without spending a cent.

Happy reading and good handling

INTRODUCTION

Do you know what is the only skill that still today 97% of people don't know that makes you make the big leap in your work and social life, and anything else?

Just wait for a second and I'll reveal everything to you. Meanwhile, I'll tell you something about me.

Just when my life seemed perfect everything fell apart.

I was a boy like everyone else who spent his days between school and that beautiful green soccer field I called home. After several years of this life, I thought it would all go well.

I would have continued to be a footballer and I already saw myself there at the top of football that counts.

But it turned out not to be like I thought.

I was almost there. I was finally auditioning for an MLS team, but during a corner kick, I looked up and saw my mother there looking at me.

I passed out as if that green grass had pulled me towards it with such a force of gravity as to drag a car. So I found myself staring at the blue sky of New York.

My father and a doctor immediately ran towards me and I woke up seeing them extremely worried, I also saw my mother in the distance crying desperately.

I knew it was over. My dreams had just been shattered. I was still a child, but I knew that my mother would never let me stay on a field again.

And so it was.

I fell into a state of depression and lost 3 years at school, My life ended at that moment.
With hindsight, however, to date, I thank my mother for the choice she made.

Without that choice of her, which I thought was wrong, I would never have met my mentor, the man from whom I learned everything I know about body language and mental manipulation of people. This discipline saved me from the abyss for its beauty and uniqueness.

So I promised myself that I would get up and take my knowledge around the world.

I went through depression and lost three years in school, traveling the world with my courses and now I'm here writing a book.

But let's get back to us. We were talking about what was the most important ability you can have today.

Surely, just if you know how to analyze the people in front of you.
But let's go step by step so as not to create confusion.

Why would anyone want to read people?

Learning how to analyze and understand the people around us is undoubtedly fundamental for two main reasons.

The first reason comes from the fact that we can immediately understand if a person is on our side or not (an enemy in short), but more simply we can understand whether someone is at ease or not, if he is afraid or not, or even if he is attracted to us, or he doesn't like us. This is only part of the things you will be able to do if you start using people analytics in your favor.

It's a bit like playing poker but knowing your opponent's cards.

Easy right? As long as you know the rules of the game. Otherwise, you will lose miserably.

The second reason is the ease you will have connecting with the people around you. You will be able to get in touch with them and relationships will become healthier, you will no longer feel like a black sheep in a pack of wolves. I never liked the similarity between black sheep and white sheep as an image.

What you learn from this book you can use as you see fit. It can be useful to you at home or work.

Think about whether you will be able to figure out what a customer wants or knowing in advance how your boss that you can't stand feels. You will have an abysmal advantage over your co-workers.

I know, you've been waiting for the promotion for a long time. Well, it's time to get it and stop just hoping it will happen one day. Hope in and of itself is not enough and is of little use. It's the action that always wins.

So if you are ready to destroy the competitors or you are tired of feeling excluded and treated badly, you must learn to understand people, and your moment of glory will not delay arriving.

Now I'm sure there are lots of questions in your head like:

- How do you do it?
- What should I watch?
- Which words should I hear and understand?

Wait a moment. Everything will be fully explained to you in the book.

But first, you need to understand the basics.

The foundations are fundamental.

This is beautiful, huh. Make a note and stick it on your fridge.

Every person nowadays wants everything at once and thinks that one thing can change their life. But, most of the time, these are bullshit, or even worse, scams. So let's go slow.

When you analyze someone you must always remember to cancel for a moment all the biases you have about that person.

If you have to analyze, for example, an acquaintance of yours that you do not tolerate, you cannot stand there thinking who he is or what he has done to you. In that case, not only will you not understand anything, but you will be more confused than before.

Take a deep breath and start observing him only for what he is doing or saying at the moment. Otherwise, you will hit a wall. Like when Willy took that red train straight on his nose in the cartoons.

You don't want to end up like that, isn't it?
Then you should listen to what this book will tell you. So you can see people's souls from their eyes and read their minds from words. This is what people who understood how to read the minds and behaviors of others did. And you will be one of them.

You will learn about all the strategies that few people know to understand, through body language and words, all the predominant characteristics of people, and how to lead them doing what you want without them noticing anything.

You will be the one to show them the way. A bit like Virgil did with Dante.

But do not get lost in chat, from now on we will enter the concrete phase of the book. Good journey.

THE BASICS OF BODY LANGUAGE

People have always expressed their feelings, sensations, and ideas through their body and their voice.

But everyone makes a severe mistake. They focus simply on the body movements of others. It is difficult for a person to know how to interpret the body.

There is a big problem that grips this aspect of the human being, which is that our words are often untrue and unrealistic.

It mast has happened to you millions of times to find yourself in this situation.

For example, a relative or a friend who tells you something you think is true but then, over time, it has turned out to be bullshit.

It is a typical situation and it happens to everyone at least once in their life. In words, we can often seem happy, sad, anxious, and so forth but body language cannot be changed and always tells the truth.

In short, knowing how to read body language makes you understand what a person thinks or wants.

(With girls it doesn't work, when they say they have nothing you don't even understand what they have from the body) Just kidding!

But how much is body language used in communication?

63% of our communication happens through the body. You may very well not believe it, but you would be wrong. For example, when a person stands with his arms folded during a discussion, HE IS NOT LISTENING TO YOU, and if you ask him, he will tell you that it is not so.

But that's a perfect action that we humans do to protect ourselves from things we don't like and think are not true.

If a person is in that position, your chances of making him change his mind are nearly 0. This gesture, like many others, does not leave room for imaginations.

I can give you other examples. If a person you are trying to understand has an arched back and their head as if it were accidentally attached to the body, well that person will surely be sad or very tired.

Everything that can be done with body language I find it fascinating.

You can be able to create new unions with people and facilitate your dialogue with them only through gestures that you previously took for granted.

While in reality, they are not like that.

But now let's move into a little more detail of what you need to do to understand the body language of the people in front of you.

The first thing to do is to figure out whether this person is comfortable with you or not in the situation he is in at that moment.

Once this step has been made and we are sure that this person has no problems at that moment with us, we must perceive the context in which we are and begin to look at the torrent of signals that bewilders us.

This of course is not easy, but with the right training and if you continue reading you will understand how to do it.

Body language is characterized by several denominators that make sure you understand if it is communicating something positive or negative to you.

Now you will have a roundup of both positive and negative body language examples to get a better idea of what I'm telling you.

Positive:

- The closeness with the person
- Feel relaxed while talking
- Look at each other for a long time
- Real smiles

Negatives:

- Feet looking at the door

- Look away

- The feeling of discomfort

- Crossed arms

- Always scratch your nose or eyes

As mentioned earlier, being with your arms folded when one speaks can mean that the person has no interest in listening to what you have to say, but this is not always the case.

It could very well mean that this person you are talking to is simply feeling uncomfortable or perhaps disappointed.

So, what I want to tell you is that you have to be careful to interpret the language because this always changes with the situation in which you find yourself.

BODY LANGUAGE CATEGORIES

There are several ways to perceive and understand which type of people are in front of you, and one of them is to understand what category this person is in. That's right people are categorized and ranked by their body language.

In total, we will see 15 different categories of people but obviously, it's not all.

Let's not get lost in small talk and let's get started.
 - Aggressive

This is the first category we see. It includes all those people who have a very threatening language, or who try to frighten the other through sudden movements.

Like when during a fight a person raises his voice a lot to frighten the other.

 - Careful

This also shows very well and is the signal that a person is working hard to achieve any goal. From studying for a task to creating the business meeting. It makes no difference. The signs are always the same.

- Bored

This is the complete opposite of the previous one. A person is bored when his eye contact is poor or completely zero.

To give you a clear example, it is like when you were in school and in class, the teacher explained something that didn't interest you at all and you began to look and focus on very stupid things like the writing on the wall but which at that moment were the best things you saw.

 - Misleading
These people are special. They often say tricks to make sure they get away with it.
But if you look carefully at them they are always worried and look around. They are very simple to understand for anyone who knows body language.

- Closed

They are all those people who are reserved and closed in on themselves. They are difficult to understand, precisely because they often do not have much body language but you recognize them by the fact that they use their arms folded not because they are not interested or tired but to protect themselves.

- Dominant

They are those people who want to be leaders in any field in their life. By themselves, they can be easily recognized by their arrogant tones and are always with the chest out.

-Defensive

These defensive people can be recognized because they are always hesitant as if they have to hide something from someone but actually, they are only afraid to expose themselves and remain alone.

- Emotional

An emotional person has very different moods during his days and is very often carried by them to act and perform actions.

- Evaluator

They are all those people who, to make a choice, evaluate all possible solutions. They do nothing on instinct but always think and never go back on their steps.

- Open

These people are always positive with everyone and are ready to accept any solution to a problem. They don't male troubles accepting what others want if they think it's right.

-Restrained

This is usually accompanied by calm and very often happy behavior. He has no strength to break the rules and always tries to respect others.

- Passionate

It is often a romantic language that expresses attraction to another person. This language is not difficult to understand as this person does not hide his interest.

- Submissive

These people very often let others humiliate them. It is very clear from body language if you are in front of such a person.

All the types of body language that have been listed for you are understandable by exemplary movements that our body communicates through poses.

Let's go back to the folded arms for a second. For example, if a person is in a meeting.

Indeed we are talking about you.

Of course, I don't know you and I don't know what your job is, but surely you will have been to a meeting or interview for a job once in your life (I hope for you that everything went well)

Well in that situation it can happen to be with your arms folded but it certainly does not mean that you are not listening, in fact, it is often the opposite and is the symbol of authoritative people who are serious.

So beware of situations.

These tips will greatly facilitate your work towards understanding people. Whatever this is (Friends, Girl / or, Parents, etc.), and so precisely understanding the situation around you will ensure that you do not waste time with messages that are actually wrong but you will focus only on the correct ones.

This will make you save hours and hours of training that you can use for something else.

Like reading my other books for example. Just kidding.

(Not too much)

However, remember to do this exercise at least 2/3 times a day. Before reading, a person analyzes the area and the situation in which you are. For the first week, avoid trying to read people but start reading situations. So everything will be easier afterward.

DO YOU KNOW WHO YOU ARE?

Great question, isn't it?

The truth is, you don't know who you are right now. I don't mean your name or surname, where you live and stuff like that.

But who you are. You need to know that 98% of people don't know why they do what they do. Wait for me to explain better. Have you ever seen someone crying in front of a painting?

The same painting might have not triggered any emotion to somebody else.

This depends on all the experiences we have been through in our lives. To understand what you have inside, you need to work on your mind and spirituality.

You don't want to hear it, but I'll tell you anyway. If you want to analyze people you must be able to analyze yourself first and understand what you have inside and why you take actions.

It will be a very hard and tiring job, at times very uncomfortable. I realize that analyzing your life is very tough, especially reliving past experiences that we don't like at all.

But we are the sum of our past experiences.

I'm not telling you to be aware of what you do all day all year round, that would be nothing short of unrealistic. But if you can do this job for 30 minutes a day it would be a big change for you.

You can do it when you prefer, I recommend that you do it in the evening before going to sleep.

You will lie down on your bed and start thinking about everything you have done during the day, give yourself explanations as to why you made that gesture or why you said that word.

This will ensure that in no time you will be able to manage your actions and your body language much better. You don't have to worry if you find it difficult for the first few days, it's perfectly normal.

Like everything in life, it takes commitment.

On the other hand, when you learned to drive you were in the same situation.

The first time you made a lot of effort and returned home with such tiredness like you have run a marathon. But now you can drive without even thinking and most of the time you do something else while driving.

For the self-reading of the body, it is the same thing. You just have to want to do it.

The first day you will feel as if a train full of people had crushed on you, but from then on the road will be all downhill.

Just want it and you can do what you want.

You need to know that your body will not be on your side. Because the mind does not want to strain, it is much easier to watch TV in the evening than to read your day. This happens mainly for two reasons, which are:

- The lack of goals
- Not knowing how the mind works

99% of the people on the planet find themselves in the first category.

People just hope that everything is fine. They don't have both short-term and long-term goals and therefore live their life randomly.

But this will get them nowhere and they will fail miserably.

Always remember murphy's law, or if something can go wrong it will. And you have to work hard to make things go your way.

So turn off that tv and chase the target.

In the second case, we also have the majority of people here. Our mind works in images, not in letters.

You may be wondering what this has to do with body language.

EVERYTHING.

If I tell you imagine yourself opening your fridge. Which side is it open on? Left to right or right to left? What color is it inside?

You are now seeing yourself in front of your fridge making movements.

It is not possible to answer these questions by heart. So you have to fool your mind.

When you do this exercise close your eyes and imagine yourself being capable of reading people and you will see that your body in a very short time will make you do all those actions that will lead you to the result you have visualized.

This should not be done once but every free moment of your day must be dedicated to this.

I know it will be tiring but if you want to succeed you have to work hard.

If you're looking for the easy way, I'm sorry for you but you got the wrong book.

Grab another one, there are plenty of people out there who want to rip you off by selling you the magic pill. You won't struggle to find any.

Now I'll be good enough to give you an exact list of ideas to understand yourself.

Certainly, it will not be easy to understand what to put where, but the beauty lies there. Otherwise, it would be too easy.

- Wishes
- Interest
- Passions
- Identity
- Thoughts
- Experienced emotions
- ideas
- Relationships
- Skills

Great, start analyzing all these about yourself. Obviously, you don't have to do it just now but rather once a day (minimum) to understand where you are going and understand all the body language well.

Feeling comfortable doing this will be impossible. For the same reasons, I explained above. But this is the only walkable way. During your research into yourself, you will truly discover who you are. But you will find it out little by little. Like when as a child you dug in the sand to find water.

You could not see it right away but had to dig deeper. First, you dug on the dry sand then slowly found the wet sand and finally the much-hidden water.

The same thing will happen to you while you are on this journey.

When this work is finally finished with clear ideas, you can throw yourself into relationships and work. Being aware of yourself will help you make well-planned career decisions.

And no longer for how you felt at the moment, but your mind will be free from thoughts and this will make you always make the best choice in more fields of your life.

THE EYES ARE THE MIRROR OF INTENTIONS

There is a saying that the eyes are the mirror of the soul. Surely, you will have heard it somewhere, perhaps from friends or at a classic Christmas dinner with the family while you were playing cards on your grandmother's table.

Where you heard it makes no difference. The important thing is that you understand that this is the case.

When we meet a person we do not know, maybe a friend of ours takes us to a party where we do not know anyone else, we will begin to look around and the first thing you will look at is people's eyes.

From them, you will understand what kind of person you are in front of but above all, the sensations he is experiencing at that moment.

If he is sad, happy, anxious, and so on.

How do we know this? Well, you must know that our pupils are a bit like those of cats.

If you have ever had one of those furry animals inside the house you will have noticed that when they walk calmly their pupils are normal, but when they hunt the black part of the eye dilates so much that almost the rest disappears.

This is because they are focused. And with the human being, it is the same thing. Our brain is capable of picking up the micro differences that occur in our pupils.
"I can see it in your eyes"

How many songs have you heard it in? Several certainly. This is because the art of understanding people from the eyes has been known for some time and also comes to us a little automatically.

The above is a very romantic and poetic sentence but at the same time dangerous.

Because the eyes moreover are the only part of the body language that cannot be manipulated. This means that people cannot lie with their eyes.

Consequently, in any situation, stare at another person's eyes and you will understand what he wants.

Reading eyes is not the easiest thing in the world and there are several ways to do it.

First of all, you don't have to let them see that you are staring into their eyes, otherwise you risk not being able to understand anything and the other person might get annoyed.

Do it "covertly" and maintain a mild and friendly contact without exaggerating.

There is a funny 1960 study done by Polt and Hess of the University of Chicago that shows just the change of the pupils.

To do this, they took a group of girls and a group of boys and placed pictures of semi-naked people in front of them.

Obviously, the girls were given pictures of men and vice versa, and believe it or not, after seeing the photos everyone's pupils, both male and female had dilated considerably.

This is certainly a fun experiment that has led to several studies on the subject over the years.

The idea of these two guys was then picked up several times in history.

As in 1966 when Kahneman (Nobel Prize in Psychology), during one of his experiments, asked all the participants to remember a series of three and seven-digit numbers by heart and then repeat them three seconds later.

The funny thing is that at the end of the experiment it was noticed that according to the length of the string of numbers the pupil dilation increased.

Funny, isn't it ?!
In short, our pupils dilate not only from excitement as seen before but also when the brain has to process information.

Are men or women better to read eyes?

The University of Cambridge has been experimenting with its pupils.

A sample of 25 boys and 25 girls were taken and they were shown photos with partly visible people's faces (eyes were present in all the photos) and asked to tell what mood the person was in the picture.

The result was that both boys and girls have excellent ability to read moods only thanks to the eyes, BUT girls did slightly better guessing 22 times out of 25 while boys only gave the correct answer 19 times.

Scientists still don't know how the brain manages to process this information. They just know we can do it.

WHERE DO WE LOOK EXACTLY AT?

There is only one way to make a true connection with a person, it happens when facing each other. According to several studies, very precise data has been obtained on where we look during a conversation.

This, of course, is not the same all over the world, for example in Japan staring a person in the eye is a sign of disrespect and aggression, therefore it is normal for them to look at the neck of the person who is speaking. Weird, isn't it?

Such a thing would be inconceivable for Italians. When someone talks, we look at them 66% of the time. Or better for 44% of the time when speaking and 73% when this person is listening.

The average duration of a glance is 2.94 seconds, that of the reciprocal glance is 1.17 seconds this reveals that during a conversation the eye contact varies from 27% to 100%. This varies depending on the speaker and the ethnicity of the interlocutors.

Therefore, before drawing your conclusions, try to understand the contest.

If you are in conversation with a Japanese, if he does not look at you it does not mean that he does it for a strange reason, but simply for his culture. While with Italians it would be exactly the opposite. So, study the situation.

CONTEXT MAKES ALL THE DIFFERENCE IN THE WORLD

In the chapter you have just finished reading, we have already talked about the importance of context with some examples, such as that of friends who are with their arms folded.

As you should know now, this does not always mean that they are bored or that they do not want to listen to you, but most likely they are tired of sitting or have eaten too much and are excessively full so try now to misread the reading of their body.

Body language is not a magic formula, like that of cartoons that will make you a gentleman in his eighties with a long white beard capable of doing who knows what fantastic magic.

I'm sorry but Dumbledore doesn't exist in everyday life. I hope I have not upset anyone ...

However, body language is not something that will make you understand for sure what people think but it will give you strong clues that, together with the context, will give you the opportunity to read people.

What is the context?

- This is a fairly difficult concept to explain and I hope to be as clear as possible.

-

- The context is the set of all the circumstances that make up the current situation. So it is made up of the environment we have around us, the words we say, the people we see and the choices made a few moments ago, this is the context.

-

- When we analyze the context it is essential to realize three fundamental things:

-

- - Spaces: When you are analyzing the context it is essential to understand the space around you. There are a lot of people, there are two of you and therefore you are alone. These differences will make the other person feel uncomfortable based on the topic you need to discuss.

–   - You need to know the recent experiences of the person in front of you: Maybe when you are talking the person in front of you has had a tough and energy-consuming day and may seem bored with you while in reality, they are just very tired.

–

–   - What we are talking about: During a conversation, especially if the tones are heated, we say hasty and pungent phrases, and maybe one of these has bothered the other interlocutor making him feel uncomfortable.

So the context is essential to understand, it will solve many problems for you if you can grasp that the problem of your conversation is due to the circumstances of the moment.

So, maybe just by changing the room or lowering the tone of the voice, you will eliminate any signs of discomfort from the other person and the conversation will go smoothly.

Sometimes, it will not be so easy to understand where the problem comes from but if for example, you come up with a topic or say a sentence which makes the person changing the mood, then you found it out, you know what bothers them. It is hard to be always so lucky, hence, at times, it will be necessary to ask directly to the person what is wrong with him.

What I just told you is the last option, however, it is possible to decrease the tension before starting to speak when for example you see that the person is already tense or upset.

Maybe offer him a cocktail or ask him how his day went so that he can open up to you and body language will not be a problem for you at that point.

Reading the context is by no means an easy practice that you will do perfectly in no time, instead, it takes a lot of training.

You can do exercises to train your reading.

When you talk to people you have a lot of confidence with, such as your parents or girlfriend, focus only on the context and not on the discussion.

In a short time, you will be able to read the context perfectly and when you find yourself in less easy situations you will deal with them without any kind of problem.

Always remember that the purpose of reading the context is to put the other person at ease and make them more open to you by also creating beautiful bonds that would never have happened without it.

Of course, your body language is also very important. If you go out of your way to understand each other but your body language isn't good for your goals, you won't get far.

You will stay right where you are waiting to read the other's body while the problem is you.

Think what a situation that could create. I advise you never to test it, unless you want to fail.

VERBAL COMMUNICATION

Verbal communication is that which occurs through languages and sounds that transmit messages that we can call "words".

These are fundamental for everyday life and it is the system with which human beings communicate. This type of communication is used between two or more people to speak in addition to body language.

Unless you are speaking with yourself... But you would need much more than this book to solve the situation.

Writing is also fundamental to verbal communication. I already see you while you think "but how?! Previously you told me that it is only the words and now also the writing." That's right my dear reader.

Writing has always been part of people's language to convey messages. Wherever you come from in the world, writing has a well-defined role.

Now, for example, are you reading but in your head, the words aren't passing as if they were written? I think so.

So writing is a part of communication but not oral. I told you that communication is words, not voice.

In this chapter, we will explore the various elements that define verbal communication and how our everyday life changes.

The foundations are fundamentals pt.2

As we have already seen before, verbal communication is all a matter of words, whether they are written or spoken does not make any difference.

But we also know that there is non-verbal communication, such as that of body language, with which we send as many messages ranging from silence to showing that we are happy.

Now, I will give you a clearer picture to make you understand better what we are talking about and the truthful distinctions that exist. You'll thank me later.

VERBAL COMUNICATION:

ORAL:

      - Spoken language

      -Movements related to suonds (laughing and crying for example)

NON-ORAL:

      - Writing or sign language

      -Gesticular or body language

Types of communication:

There are two types of communications, they are public speaking and interpersonal communication.

These two are the two main types of communication that we all use during our days but they have some nice differences between them.

The first usually refers to communication between you and a large number of people who listen, while the second is done the same with a group of people but these do not just listen to you, they also exchange opinions.

I'll give you two examples to make things clearer.

The first case could be a speech that the teacher gives in the classroom while talking about the Second World War, the students are good (in theory) to listen to what the teacher is explaining to them.

In the second case, let's always take the school as an example, an interpersonal conversation could be a question where the teacher and the pupil talk to each other, hoping that the latter would reply.

Communication is always a challenge. More with ourselves than with others.

We certainly have more challenges with verbal communication than with non-verbal communication. Whenever we find ourselves in a speech, finding the right words is often hard.

This happens either because the two people who are talking have completely different ideas as it can happen if two religious extremists find themselves arguing or because the message has not been transmitted well and this means that the communication is broken and not functional.

A good piece of advice I can give you is 10 seconds.

But I think you all know that you should stop 10 seconds before speaking, this to ponder well on what needs to be said and how to say it above all, without anyone getting offended.

Surely it has already happened to you two hundred thousand times that after a conversation you think "But why did I say this" or "But how did I talk to him?".

Well, this happens to all of us but you can reduce the number of times this thing happens with this simple trick.

Each one of us expresses himself differently, and we cannot command others but we absolutely can.

For this, we need to know how to use all kinds of language to let the best side of us pass and decide exactly what comes out of our mouth without having bad surprises during the discussion.

Another fundamental part of communication is given by symbols.

Symbols certainly deserve to be dealt with in the chapter on verbal communication.

What are them specifically?

Symbols are thoughts, objects, ideas, and emotions. They are all we need to give meaning to our actions. Symbols are never without meaning but always have a reason.

The symbols are characterized by different qualities and are also defined by the 3 "a" rule, they are the following:

- Ambiguous
- Abstract
- Arbitrary

The most obvious example we can give today to describe the ambiguous symbols is certainly "Apple" in fact today this word has taken on more meanings. To understand it better, I'll give you an example.

When you read apple did you think about an apple or an electronics brand?

Precisely this I mean with ambiguous. It is not known exactly what we are indicating with that word. But we have to see the context in which it is inserted to understand.

The meaning of the symbols is constantly changing and it will be as long as the human being is on earth and this thanks to the continuous social changes and discoveries that will make today's language obsolete in twenty years.

Just look at the new generations with the old ones. To date, children speak a language that parents do not understand and have different symbols.

In the second point, we have abstraction. Abstract symbols are used to convey an intricate concept directly and simply.

A classic example on this topic is when talking to the "public", this is an abstraction because we don't know how to quantify the people present and we don't even know what they are like, what ethnicity, etc.

But we all have in our minds a more or less abstract idea of an audience, ranging from those in the cinema to the myriad of people who find themselves inside an arena for the Lakers playoffs.

In short, a symbol is abstract when we cannot define only through what we are talking about specifically but we need more information.

Lastly, there are arbitrary symbols, that is, they are all those symbols that have no direct correlation with what we want to talk about but that helps us communicate the concept we want to express.

PEOPLE BEHAVE ALL THE SAME WAY

Human behavior is extremely hard to be interpreted, but there is a point in our favor that will always help us in our reading, that is, all human beings react similarly on some occasions and leave no room for uncertainty.

For scientists, human behavior has always been divided into three well-defined components which are action, emotion, and cognition.

Let's start talking about the first topic, the action. Actions are all those movements that carry out a behavior that makes you move from one situation to another. A trivial example occurs when you go to sleep.

You decide to change your position and to do so you take an action.

In the second position, we find knowledge.

These are described as images that we create in our heads. They can be both verbal and non-verbal.

Those verbal can be said all those knowledge that we tell another person on any subject.

"I wonder what it will be like to drive that flaming yellow Lamborghini" This, for example, is a verbal knowledge.

While when you think about how you will be in ten years, well that is non-verbal cognition because you are just imagining in your head and you are not talking to anyone.

Last but certainly not least we find emotions.

These are all those short experiences that we live without reasoning, they too are divided into two large groups that we are going to understand and they are positive and negative.

We cannot change our emotions because they take us by surprise and our bodies cannot help but behave in a certain way.

Like when your favorite team is in the final and close to the end, but there is a shot of 2 that could make you win the game, without a doubt you will have your heart racing. These actions cannot be controlled because they are dictated by emotion.

The same thing happens with the negative emotions you experience (I hope for you they never happen to you) at a funeral. The negative emotions you will feel in there cannot be controlled by the mind.

Whether they are good or bad, emotions cannot be stopped.

The set of emotions, actions, and cognitions makes us understand the situation that surrounds us and together these three things make our life full. Without them, nothing you will do will make sense.

These three things often occur at the same time and follow this equation:

Action = Emotion + Cognition

For example, if you are sitting at the bar and you get up to pay but while you walk to the checkout you see a dear friend of yours, you have just completed all three phases.

You got up and did an action, you saw your friend and you felt a joy so you used your cognition and emotions.

Very often during our life, we use these behaviors but we don't realize them. Now that you know it you will surely pay attention to it and you will be able to recognize the situation without hesitation.

THE POWER OF HANDS

The hands have a power that we do not know at all and we ignore. They send a huge number of messages that most people can't get.

Hands have always been used in conversation and their meaning has changed countless times over the years. An example is a handshake.

The act of shaking hands finds its roots in the past. When the ancient tribes met they used to show their palms to show that they were not hiding anything.

The Roman Empire instead used to tighten the forearm so both people were sure that the other did not hide anything under his sleeve. This was done because in those days it was normal going around with a knife under the sleeve and to be safe they adopted this habit.

But like all the customs that have passed from generation to generation to date, the one used by the Romans has turned into our handshake.

This gesture for us is used in a myriad of different situations. Ranging from the classic greeting with friends to a handshake to establish a working agreement between two large multinationals.

Even in Japan, where the classic greeting has always been the bow, today the handshake is widely used.

The fact that it is now a widespread gesture does not mean that it is simple to do. Behind the handshake, there is a real world of domination and submission.

Still, in ancient Rome, two people greeted each other with an arm-wrestling handshake, I define it.

In other words, it was not common to shake hands as we do today, but one person took the hand of the other from bottom to top and created the shape of a sandwich so to speak. The most powerful person dominated the other.

Nowadays this practice is not used but the person you win always exists while handshaking. There are three different types of endings for a handshake which are:

- Dominance
- Submission
- Equality

These attitudes are perceived at the unconscious level and our body processes them in a particular way and each of these can decide in which direction the conversation will go.

An example I can give you is that of a study done on some company managers.

Male or female makes no difference.

It has shown that 89% of them use the dominant handshake and always hold out their hand first, so they can control the handshake accurately.

The exact opposite is submissive handshake. In this case, the person puts his hand palm up, granting the other person dominance. A bit like dogs do when they lie down and put their bellies to the sky.

You can use this handshake if you want your interlocutor to feel in control of the situation. You can use this squeeze when you go to make excuses for example.

On the other hand, when the two people are in a position in which both want to turn the other's hand to dominate, what is called a "bite" is created, which causes the people to be equal and neither of them, in the end, gets the better.

So, if you want to create an equal relationship with the person in front of you, avoid him turning your hand, but most importantly, use the same amount of force that he uses.

Now let's use hypothetical numbers, if he applies a force of 9 out of 10 to the handshake and you of apply one of 7 out of 10, you will have to increase the strength or you will be dominated. The same thing you will have to do in reverse if you don't want to dominate.

In short, if he applies a force of 5 and you of 7 if you do not want to be seen dominant you will have to forcefully lower the power of your grip.

But now I'll tell you a trick to never let yourself be dominated. Not even if you were to meet the president of the united states.

Indeed with this technique, you will always and I repeat always dominate the other (always if in that situation you want to do it).

The technique is called "disarming the doers"
The technique consists of putting the arm outstretched with the palm facing down so as not to leave any escape for your interlocutor and he will have to forcefully turn his hand and put himself in submission.

From that moment on, you can do whatever you want. You decide whether to dominate or be equal but it will be very difficult for him to bring the situation in his favor.

A bit like it happens in games when you are three points above your antagonist and the game is about to finish, he has to do a miracle to win, indeed the options for him are to draw or to lose.

If, on the other hand, you happen to find yourself in the situation where a person holds out his hand as described above, there is something you can do to reverse the situation.

Step forward with your left foot and make sure to bring his hand vertically. This practice is not simple because we tend to advance with the right, but with a little training, you will see that it will come more than natural to you.

If you really can't take this step there is another way to save yourself from domination and that is the double catch.

When the other brings you to palm up, you use the other hand which is free to return the hold to a tie. So right now you are using two hands while he is using just one.

Staying on the left is an unfair advantage

During a handshake, the position you are in is crucial, and staying on the left helps a lot if you want to dominate.

This happens because on the right you have no control over the situation, while on the left you can actually do it.

Kennedy liked this technique very much, even if at that time nothing was known about body language, he already applied it by intuition.

If you go to see all the photos where he meets with leaders and famous people you will always find him on the left with the double grip.

A striking example of how Kennedy was a phenomenon with body language is when he won the election against Nixon.

That time it was noted that the people who only heard the speeches of the two politicians were convinced that Nixon had won while those who watched the scene agreed otherwise.

This led Kennedy to win the election. Pretty important this body language, isn't it?

Going back to the speech above, however, if you are on the right of the photo to be able to have an equal situation, reach out to force him to shake your hand as you want.

To conclude this chapter, I give you a summary.

Few people know what an impression they can make on a stranger, even if they are aware of how important it is to have a great starting point in a conversation.

Take some time to experiment with the various handshakes with perhaps friends, relatives, or work colleagues to get familiar with it, so that during important moments you will know how to behave correctly.

BEHIND THE MAGIC OF A SMILE

Laughter has always been seen as a sign of happiness.

What if I told you it's not always the case?

Young children quickly learn that laughter is something that fascinates older children and they use it to their advantage. Like the crying phase, it works the same way.

But several studies show that laughter in nature is used for multiple purposes. Let's look at our ancestors, the monkeys, for example.

These animals have two types of smiles that are completely different from each other. The first is that in which the animal shows itself inferior and to do so they show all the teeth but lower the sides of the mouth.

The movement is very similar to that of the laughter of human beings to make it clearer.

While the second smile is used to show the other animal that he is aggressive and could bite. To do this, the monkey shows his teeth completely but also spreads his jaws apart. To date we no longer do this but humans also use laughter in different ways.

Do you have a contagious smile?

A smile is something very special. In fact, when a person smiles at you you are forced to reciprocate. Your body does it automatically without you noticing.

Even if it's a fake smile.

A study done by a university in Sweden shows how our body responds to smiling. 130 volunteers were taken and placed one by one in front of slides where you could see images of people laughing, crying, and getting angry.

The funny thing was the result. Because each one of them was asked to do the opposite face to what they saw.

If they saw a cry they had to laugh and so on. On each of them was installed a machine that detected the micro signals of their body.

It was noticed that when they saw an image of a person crying, they had no hesitation in making a smiling face. While when the photo appeared with a laugh, the instinct of the person who tried the experiment was to smile.

Of course, this gesture was almost invisible to the human eye but thanks to those particular machines they were able to detect the contagiousness of the smile.

The difficult thing to understand is whether a smile is sincere or not. Our mind cannot tell the difference when we get one.

Most people have a sense of happiness when they receive a smile, even if this is true or false. A characteristic that distinguishes a fake smile is that it is often done from only one side of the mouth.

If you see someone smiling at you so, be careful, 99% of them are lying.

According to some studies, however, it appears that those who tell lies smile little or much less. This happens because our body knows that if we fake laugh the other person notices this situation and will get caught.

But when it happens that a liar laughs his smile has a much longer duration than the average.

It remains printed as a kind of mask. It is no coincidence that in some movies the villain has a smile on his face. A classic example is that of Joker.

The choice of the mask is not accidental. The creators of batman knew this characteristic of villains very well and put it into practice in the best possible way.

The Smile Heals

The smile has a prodigious effect on our body, it can produce natural "pain relievers" capable of destroying some diseases in our body.

Do you know who Norman Cousins is?

No? Well, I tell you. This person has started countless studies on the effect that the smile has on our body.

One day, through a medical check-up, he was diagnosed with a disease that would soon make him feel unbearable pain in his bones and it would get worse and worse.

Anyone would have shut themselves up in the house crying and despairing.

But for him, this could not be done.

He went to a DVD store and I bought all the funniest movies he found on the shelf, he came home and started watching all these movies and laughed as hard as he could. After a few weeks, she went back to the doctor who was amazed.

Not only was the disease gone but he hadn't felt the slightest physical pain.

From then on, a myriad of studies on the incident began and it was discovered that laughing has the same effect that morphine could have.

So in the early eighties, hospitals began to open what was called "rice rooms".

In these rooms magazines, movies, and funny characters were inserted and patients were brought in for at least an hour a day and of course, the results did not hesitate to arrive.

Even today this practice helps a myriad of people around the world.

This easily explains why when a person who laughs a lot looks better and gets sick much less than a person who always complains or is sad for any reason.

WHAT HAVE IN COMMON LAUGHTER AND CRYING?

Laughter and crying are closely linked to each other both from a physiological and a psychological point of view.

Experiment on yourself. Try to remember the last time you laughed a lot at a joke or whatever.

You almost felt goose bumps, isn't it?

Those are the endorphins that our body releases without us knowing it after a real laugh. That feeling is similar to what people who take drugs of any kind have.

85% of those who have problems laughing at the good things in life fall victim to alcohol or drug abuse. Because these substances make it possible to laugh and relax "faster" according to their concept.

People who use these substances fall into two large groups.

The first is that of people who are already happy and increase their happiness by taking endorphins.

The second group is that of people who are unhappy, but if they overdo these substances instead of becoming happy they risk turning into dangerous and violent people or become desperate.

. . ..

People drink alcohol and take drugs in an attempt to feel like someone who is happy

....

At the end of this chapter, I would like to give you a suggestion. Laugh in your life. You will improve relationships with people you just met and also with those you already know. You will be facilitated at work and in sport. You will strengthen your immune system and you will be able to read people better as they will be more open to you.

Humor is a lifesaver !!

ARMS TELL

During a person's life, body language changes over the years. A little like what happens with our personality, it becomes more and more sophisticated.

A prime example of what I just told you is your arms.

When we are children we do not take into account our body language and to protect ourselves we hide behind the first thing that happens when we are afraid.

You will surely have seen a child make this gesture. Or maybe you still have clear childhood memories of yourself doing it.

Like when you hid under the bed to escape monsters.

However, at the age of six, this no longer happens and instead of running away, we cross our arms very hard when we feel we are in danger or in a situation that we do not like.

Growing up even more than when we are in adolescence, our arms in those situations remain softer but for example, we tend to cross our legs.

We do this gesture of bringing our arms to our chest for a very specific reason, and it is a legacy that we carry from the past.

The reason is that we protect our vital organs if we feel threatened. If you notice when you cross your hands you put them at the height of the heart and lungs.

And no, it's not by chance.

This gesture, however, in some situations has been studied which leads to very visible disadvantages.

A very clear example is that of an experiment that was conducted in the United States in a university. Two different groups were created to attend a convention.

The first group was told to see the whole convention without being able to cross their arms in any way. So they had to hold them along the body.

While the other group was told to cross its arms obligatorily for the duration of the lesson.

At the end of it, a test was done to see which group had better assimilated the information acquired.

The result was shocking, to say the least. The group with the arms along the body had absorbed nearly forty percent more of the information that had been explained to them.

While the other group not only found themselves struggling with the task but also questioned the person who had given the lesson.

What I just told you was not the only experiment that has been done on these topics but all the other tests done have brought to similar results to what I have just described to you.

Some people, however, for example, tend to say "yes but I'm comfortable like this". The problem is that any gesture is convenient when we find ourselves having that attitude.

If you find yourself in an uncomfortable situation and cross your arms, you will feel comfortable. But if you do it at a friend's house, you may be giving the wrong message even if it's not your intention.

Always remember that all body messages you give make sense not only for you but also for the people around you.

The lesson is very clear from my point of view. Arms should never be crossed unless you want to communicate that you disagree or that you are stranger to the situation.

This lesson also applies in reverse.

Let me say that better. I have no idea who you are, but if you are reading this book you are interested in body language. So I want to give you a little trick to make sure you don't have to find yourself talking to someone who has their arms folded.

There is just one solution. For example, if during a meeting in which you are explaining the projects that will be implemented shortly thereafter you notice that a collaborator is in the position of folded arms give him something to do.

Yes, you got it right. You have to make sure he cannot stay in that position, and to do so you would give him something in his hand or maybe have him write something or even better say "Do you want to say something? If so, please stand up."
In short, do whatever you can to get him changing that position.

Types of crossed arms

Crossed arms don't always reveal the same things. But you may encounter several situations which are as follows:
- Arms folded and closed fist
- Grip on arms
- Thumbs up
- The position of the broken zip

When a person is in the first position, that is with his arms folded and his fists closed, undoubtedly he is feeling strong disapproval and in the worst-case scenario, one can expect a verbal and even physical attack from this person. So it's best to immediately understand where the problem lies and fix it.

In the second case, however, the grip of the arms represents your uncertainty of what you are about to do.

When we are in the waiting room at the dentist or we are about to get on the plane if we are afraid of flying. Here in these situations, people use this behavior to feel more protected.

In the third case, we find the position with the arms crossed but with the thumbs upwards.

In this case, the situation is very different. This type of position is taken by all those self-confident people during an interview, for example.

So if you want to appear confident, take this position and you will see that things would change right away.

Lastly, we find the position of the broken zip. Nice name, don't you think?

In this position, we put all those people who are sad and by nature protect the genitals from possible frontal attacks.

This position calls discouragingly and a lot of vulnerability. It is often used by people, for example, queuing for benefits or asking for charity.

How the rich show their insecurities

Famous people also feel under pressure and not at ease in the crowd. They are just good at not showing it.

Or rather they know how to move and have figured out how to avoid it being noticed.

Certainly, they cannot be seen as insecure and agitated, don't you think?

If the politician on duty showed that he was under pressure at a conference, no one would follow him and he certainly wouldn't make a career.

Usually, instead of crossing their arms, they use to touch the bracelets or cuffs of the jacket. It is still a safety barrier but much less visible.

A striking example of a person using this technique is Prince Charles.

Pay attention to it. Take videos of getting out of his car with the driver and approaching the crowd. You will see that every time he touches the cufflinks of the shirt.

Yet one should think "but he is used to seeing a lot of people".

It doesn't matter. Human beings try to avoid finding themselves in a situation where they are in danger.

This was just an example, but an anxious and uncomfortable man may touch the strap of his watch or maybe rub his hands or play with the button on his jacket but he will certainly not sit still.

Another example can be that of businessmen. When they head into a meeting room they usually hold the suitcase on their chest.

This behavior only names one thing. ANXIETY.

It doesn't matter in what situation or context it happens but being with folded arms is taken with negativity.

What then the message affects both people in conversation. Even if your back simply hurts, the other will perceive it as a negative gesture.

So train NOT to cross your arms. Unless you want to point out a situation that you think is wrong.

DAILY GESTURES AND THEIR MEANING

There are many movements and gestures that we are sometimes forced to do but that we will never want to do.

I'll give you a quick example so you can understand what I mean.

Do you know what it means when two people hug each other and one of them starts patting the other one on the back?

In most cases, it may seem like a matter of affection but it's not the case, indeed this is the opposite situation.

In reality, these taps have the same meaning that we can find in boxing, that is the end of the match.

When a person makes this gesture, it means that he wants to get out of that situation as soon as possible.

This is only one of the examples that we will analyze in this chapter where you will discover many things about everyday human behavior.

The positions of the head

Let's start by talking about the movements and the position in which we put our heads to send messages.

The main positions for the head used by men are three
- Straight ahead
- Inclined
- Bent over

In the first case, or when a person keeps his head straight towards the interlocutor, it mainly means that he is having a neutral attitude towards who is talking or what he is saying.

The same position is exchanged at times as if the person was deciding what he feels. This is sometimes true but it is not always the case.

If, on the other hand, you notice that the person starts to raise his chin and consequently his head is sending you clear messages where he tells you that he feels superior to you and wants to dominate the conversation.

By putting themselves in that position, people have the impression of putting themselves higher than everyone else and thus can give the impression of looking down on everyone.

This position is a bit of a challenge.

In the second case, we find the tilted head. This position occurs when a person turns their head to either the right or left side.

When you see this situation it means that the person is submitting. He is showing his neck and throat and that makes him look weak.

This attitude owned by human bodies comes from our childhood and put our little head on the shoulder of our parents. We showed ourselves helpless and had them do the protective work.

But this position is not used just in negative moments.

Many studies show that women, for example, use this technique much more than men to seduce. Man has always felt attracted to women who seem to be non-threatening and show signs of submission.

This is also noticeable in advertisements where it is often put in that position.

Just think of all those commercials where models try on clothes or have to sell things. The next time you have one of these advertisements under your eyes, pay attention to it.

This does not mean that women are inferior. Indeed they are very good at using this game in their favor and make men do whatever they want.

Consequently, if you are holding a meeting or exposing something, pay attention to all people who put their necks to the side. If they are many, it means that what you are saying works 100%.

Finally, we find the sign of the bowed head.

When you see that a person is in this position, you have to be careful. As the one who is listening is in a very critical situation and a negative attitude.

If the person stays with his head bowed, your chances of communicating something with him are practically zero.

Many people who work in sales or show business very often find themselves struggling with such attitudes.

To date, however, "solutions" have been found if they can be called so to get rid of this position from the person. For example, in the entertainment world, you interact much more with the public hoping that they are more attentive to what you are saying.

Human beings use their head to send out many other warnings that we do not perceive.

One of them is the nod.

In most countries of the world, this gesture means either an affirmative answer and therefore we are on the same side as the interlocutor or it can mean a hint of a bow. A partial bow.

Bowing since it was first done has always been a sign of submission. It was used in ancient times to venerate gods or emperors.

Much researches conducted on body language have shown that even those with perceptual disabilities, therefore blind, deaf, and dumb, use this particular gesture to say yes.

It is curious that a person who has never seen uses his head to say yes or no, don't you think?

This happens because these gestures are within us. Body language is not created or learned, we already have it within us at birth. Of course, you can control it but we just know certain gestures.

Pay attention to the country or place where you are.

What one thing means to us does not always apply to others. In India, for example, it is not conventional to nod as we do but they swing their heads side to side.

Yes, that's what I said. They use the gesture we make to say "so and so" to say "yes". There is a myriad of these examples that I could give you but one more would be sufficient.

In Japan, for example, nodding is not used to say yes but to say "ok, I'm listening to you". Sometimes this also happens to us but not always while for them this is how it is done.

The nod of the head has its origins in the act of submission

I have a test for you. Can you tell if a person who nods to you wants you to keep talking or not?

I assumed the answer is no. Don't worry, no one out there knows this information.

While talking with someone, especially if you are the speaker, you need to know how to interpret other people's body language.

When you find yourself in conversation, the person you are talking to in 86% of cases will nod his head. Don't think this is always a positive sign, you have to look at the speed with which he nods.

If during the conversation the person nods to you slowly, it means that he is interested in what you are saying, but if on the contrary, he nods quickly his only thought is " when does he stop talking about these things? "

Unfortunately, this is reality. So if you find yourself in this situation, look at the details.

POWER GAMES

Have you ever gone to a job interview and left after an hour without having the job?

Probably you did it. Following the 1587 pieces of research done in this field, it has been found that there is a strong correlation between being appreciated by the person who is offering you the chance to get a job and getting the position for real.

It often ends up that all the sheets you have prepared as a resume are sent to the trash and during the interview, you are asked to talk about things far from your competences.

What the interviewer will remember of you is just the impression you gave him.

……..

In the world of work, the first impression is like love at first sight

……..

No worries, here I am to save you from waste another chance or, even better, you could get yourself a nice promotion by applying what you will find below.

You are about to read The Nine Commandments to make a good impression.

THE NINE RULES OF INESTIMABLE VALUE TO MAKE A GOOD IMPRESSION.

Let's pretend that from now on you will have to face a job interview. You should know that the first impression is already made after the first four minutes of conversation.

65/87% of your impact will be given by non-verbal language. So pay attention to your behavior.

The situations you will encounter are the following.

- Waiting room
- Entrance
- Approach
- Handshake

- Sitting down
- The place where you sit
- The gestures
- The distance
- The exit

These are the fundamental points that you will have to face to do an excellent interview.

But let's get straight into the explanation.

The waiting room: The first thing to do is to take off your coat and maybe give it to the receptionist or in any case remove all those objects that could make you look too clumsy.

So don't come in with 289 bags. Unless you want to give a bad impression.

Another crucial thing is not to sit in the waiting room. The receptionist will insist on letting you sit down but she only does it because if you are seated she can forget about you.

Stand and wait with your arms behind your body.

The entrance: The time will come when the receptionist will let you into the boss's office or at least show you the door.

You must enter fearlessly keeping the same pace you were using previously. Do not slow down and do not take small steps otherwise you will look scared.

This is what you want to avoid, isn't it?

The approach: Here the issues start. The person you need to talk to for any reason is distracted. Maybe he's drinking or his pencil has fallen out. You go straight on, put your suitcase or whatever you have with you, and sit down.

Don't waste your time otherwise, you look like someone who is looking for a job but they don't know what to do.

Which may be true but you don't have to show it.

Handshake: Keep your hand straight and don't give up. Use the same strength he is putting into it.

Please don't shake your hand over the desk but go left. This way you will have a strong hand at your disposal and you will not find yourself giving your palm down.

Sitting down: This part is very important and should not be underestimated. You will usually be placed in a lower chair than the bosses.

But you turn it to the side 45 degrees if it can't get up. So you don't have to stay in the "prayer" position.

The place where you sit: If they make you talk in an informal place like a corridor or maybe outdoor, you have to be happy for two reasons.

The first one is that 99% of no's during interviews are said from behind a desk. The other reason is that by standing you can safely control your whole body.

Gesture: make slow and sharp movements. Always remember that if you want to be seen as a person of substance you must not gesticulate or rather if you have to do it slowly.

This is a legacy that we have been carrying around for many years and derives from the sale of objects. You will wonder how this is possible.

But that's exactly how it is. In ancient times the poor used to gesticulate much more to sell their products.

While the rich and the bosses often didn't even have to talk many times to get others to do what they wanted.

Distance: Always remember to maintain adequate distances between people.

If this is the first time you meet someone, keep at least one meter from him or even more. This will ensure you won't feel under pressure.

You can easily tell from his body language if what you are leaving is the right space.

Many people when in front of a desk start tapping their fingers on them.

Also, pay attention to the age of the person you are talking to. If this is the same age as you then you can be closer but if he is older, the distance increases.

The Exit: When you come to this moment take all your belongings calmly and go out.

But watch out for the door. If when you entered someone closed it then you will do the same otherwise leave it as it is.

When you go out, be careful not to give the impression of being clumsy and watch out the back of the shoes.

It must always be clean. You'd be impressed by how many people unconsciously look at this particular aspect.

If you are a woman and you have talked to a man this will stare at you while leaving...you guess where.
They don't do it maliciously.

But you turn around and smile once at the door. It is more important that they remember your face rather than the b-side.

IS IT CLEAR WHEN WE LIE?

I know you've always wondered. Many people come to this interrogative during their lifetime

Can you tell lies without being seen?

The answer is yes. But you have to be very careful about how you speak. When you lie, our body gives signs to the interlocutor that make him understand the truth.

These signs range from sweating in the palms to small tics in the cheeks.

In order not to make it clear that you are lying, you must truly believe in what you are saying. Even if it's all fake.

CAUTION. With this, I am not advising you to lie.

I'm telling you that it is possible to do it but you have to be excellent "actors".

To understand if the "good lie" exists or not, scientists have taken some birds for experiments.

Birds with dark plumage are always the leaders. Those who eat earlier and take less risk.

So the scientists took some light birds and colored them dark to see if they could become the pack leader.

You can already imagine how it turned out. None of them had any improvements.

Do you know why?

Because they have changed color but have not changed their behavior and the other animals still perceived these weaknesses inside them and this experiment did not change anything.

I told you this story to make you understand that reading this book once will not be enough to fully understand people.

It takes training to do anything right.

Do not take everything for granted. When you are at home instead of wasting time watching the tv, look at your parent's moves or instead watch a movie and pay attention to the movements of the actors in various situations.Increasing concentrationand draw strength.

Every day we accumulate tension and are forced to constantly perform.performance. "Doing nothing" or simply remaining relaxed is a state we are no longer very a state to which we are no longer very accustomed.
But being able to find a balanced relationship between tension and relaxation is vital in life. This theme of the month focuses on different methods of relaxation.

In all vital systems, phases of intense activity alternate with quieter phases. Contraction and relaxation, tension and relaxation, or systole and diastole are just examples that relate directly to our motor system.

that relate directly to our motor system. In this context, it is important to make rhythmic change.

In training and physical education there are many possibilities to In training and physical education there are many possibilities to integrate a game of alternating between performing, releasing tension or moving and relaxing. and relaxing.

In sport, moments of relaxation can play a decisive role. Muscle tension, stress and psychic pressure impair sporting performance.

It is a question of avoiding reactions that reduce performance and, if such reactions do occur, to be able to manage them and to be aware of their consequences and, if they do occur, to be able to manage and counteract them as best you can.

Instructions and films This month's theme focuses on relaxation in adult sport.
However, the measures listed can also be used and adapted accordingly for young people and children.
The first part contains background information on the topic of relaxation. Afterwards, you will find and answers to questions such as: "What do I need to pay attention to?
How do I introduce a relaxation phase?", "How do I end a relaxation session correctly?".

The proposed breathing and relaxation exercises can be integrated into daily life or to lighten up the lessons.
or to lighten up the lessons.

In addition, they are ideal for a return to calm during sports lessons in the snow, at the gym or in the woods.

in the snow, in the gym or in the forest. Two teaching aids will also be presented for use training or during physical education lessons: the relaxation dice and the set of cards for a relaxation trail.Relaxation methods can play an important role in sport.

sport. When applied in a targeted manner, they serve to develop balance, speed up regeneration and improve self-control.
A number of well-dosed relaxation methods can be useful in the following areasduring training or physical education.

Concentration

Commonly, concentration is often equated with mental effort that can lead to bodily tension.

lead to bodily tension. Today, however, it is known that attention reaches its highest levels when one is in a state of mental alertness.

levels when one is in a relaxed and loose state. For this reason, it is recommended to include relaxation phases before, after and between the individual training units.

Regeneration With the help of targeted relaxation, you can accelerate regeneration after training or competition.

training or a competition. Relaxation also allows you to take a short break and regenerate during breaks in competitions or if there are delays, without losing all tension.

without losing tension completely.

Quality of movement The prerequisite for a technically optimal conduct of movements is the alternation between tension and relaxation.

between tension and relaxation. Through regular practice of relaxation methods, a sensitivity is the difference between tense and relaxed muscles.

and relaxed. In this way, you can improve your overall perception of your body.

body. Differentiated physical perception supports learning and makes it easier to correct movement sequences.

correction of movement sequences.

Psychoregulation
While preparing for a performance, it is possible to learn self-regulation techniques with the help of suitable mental and physical exercises.

mental and physical exercises, it is possible to learn self-regulation techniques.

level of activation for training or competition. Relaxation is an important part of these regulation processes. In addition, it forms the basis of otherskills useful for self-regulation (imagination, gymnastics with alternating play of tension and relaxation, progressive muscle relaxation to reduce nervousness).

Imagination

Imagining a sequence of movements consciously and intensively helps to later improve the actual movements.

The ability to relax is a fundamental prerequisite for the successful implementation of mental training of this kind.

forms of mental training of this kind. It is therefore useful to systematically reach a relaxed state before and after visualising the movements.b and after visualising the movements. What should you pay attention to when integrating a relaxation session into a training session?

How do you give instructions to achieve relaxation?

How do you finish the sequence?

Here are some points to ideal relaxation.

Effective training also contains relaxation sequences. It makes sense to perform It makes sense to perform these sequences in a correct rhythm and to introduce and carry them out in this way.

Therefore, it is important to take several points into consideration.

Introduction and preparation

Effort and performance orientation block the development of a relaxed reaction.

relaxed reaction.

The aim of the introductory phase is to reduce the level of activity achieved by the previous exercises.

previous exercises. For this purpose simple exercises that prepare you for relaxation, such as to relaxation, such as regulating and slowing down the breathing rhythm, relaxing the muscles and calming eye movements (including eyelids).

External conditions

As the perception limit is reduced during relaxation, it is useful, especially for beginners, to exclude external influences.

beginners, it is useful to exclude disturbing external influences. By preparing suitable by preparing suitable external conditions, one can avoid unpleasant frights which could also have physical side effects.

Relaxation process

In the initial phase of a relaxation process, the outward-looking attention

In the initial phase of a relaxation process, outward-facing attention is transformed into a passive form of inward-facing perception.

With the exception of progressive muscle relaxation, many other relaxation methods aim to achieve a state of relaxation.

with the exception of progressive muscle relaxation, the aim is to achieve a state of calm. Through self-instruction, repetition of phrases repetition of phrases or observation of the breathing rhythm, it is possible to strengthen the direct attention on inner perception.

on internal perception. The reduction of external stimuli slowly leads to the reduction in the intensity of attention and neuromuscular tone.
In order to reduce the neuromuscular tone even more, it is important that mental activities related to the imagery of movements are also abandoned.

It is useful to exercise regularly and under the same conditions until the relaxation reaction is consolidated and leads to a more relaxed reaction.

consolidated and leads to a conditioned reaction. With increasing experience
physiological changes occur with such regularity that they are interpreted as subjective indicators of success.
as subjective indicators of success.

Tendency to fall asleep

The natural tendency to fall asleep during a relaxation exercise can become an obstacle while learning.

become an obstacle while learning a method. Therefore, it is necessary to reduce the factors

Therefore, the factors that can lead to falling asleep should be reduced, avoiding too long units, sleep-like body positions, times of the day when one already feels tired anyway
and reduced stimulation due to lack of instruction.Do you breathe through your nose or mouth?

When does breathing have a calming or stimulating effect?

The following is an overview with the most important points about breathing.

Favour nasal breathing: When you are calm, it is best to breathe through the nose.

Nasal breathing promotes good basic relaxation of the entire organism, encourages diaphragm activity and leads to a deeper inhalation.

During a stronger inhalation, the nostrils are muscularly activated and the inner nasal cavities are enlarged.
are enlarged.

Only when the overload increases, the mouth is also used.

Well-balanced tone: the body's posture is the result of a dynamic interplay between the skeleton, muscles and the influence of gravity.

To achieve good posture

To achieve good posture, the respective muscles need only to maintain balance in a dynamic manner.

To achieve such a state, basic muscle tension is sufficient.
well dosed. Thus, the muscles are able to give space for
breathing movements at any time and in all directions.

any time and in all directions, even in the back.
Under these conditions, breathing takes place efficiently and
economically.

The more

posture is bad, the more the muscles are busy holding the body
position or balancing its tendencies.

body position or balance its tendencies. For this reason, the
muscles cannot be relaxed completely to give
make room for breathing movements.

Breathing activity increases, breathing becomes demanding
becomes demanding and only works in a limited way.

CONCLUSION

By reading this book you will have understood many things about body language and manipulation that you did not know before.

All people when they are in front of an interlocutor very often leave out revealing details.

They see them only if they are pointed out to them. We are all similar to a deaf person who is told to take something but until it is not shown he will never be able to grasp what is happening.

Body language, or non-verbal language, has existed since the dawn of time.

But science only focused on it at the end of the twentieth century.

During the past years, the studies made have been numerous and many of which you have read here.

This has become a real discipline that today is included in many courses of university and non-university institutes.

A lot of people study the discipline out of curiosity and others to use it in their favor.

A past student of mine named Alex was able to take a corporate award in three months since he applied what I taught him.

He came to me out of desperation. After several years on the sidelines of the company where he worked, he was tired of that situation and no longer wanted to see people who passed him constantly.

So he "applied" everything and changed his life.

I did not write the word to apply by chance.

I already know that at least 50% of the people who read this book will not take a minute to apply and test the concepts explained.

Many will not even get to this point.

Too bad for them, but I congratulate you on at least making it this far.

From now on the difficulties begin.

Don't be like the others who put this book on the shelf and in a few days forget everything leaving the book gathering dust.

Do not do it. Believe in yourself and that you can do it.

Take at least thirty minutes a day to organize your workouts and re-read the concepts you see that you have forgotten.

If you have an interview or something important at work, re-read the essential chapters.

But above all apply them.

This is the key part.

My teachings FOR THE MOMENT END HERE.

I wish you good training and await your feedback of success.